The In Between

Analise Emmerick

BookLeaf Publishing

India | USA | UK

Presentation by *BookLeaf Publishing*

Web: www.bookleafpub.com

E-mail: info@bookleafpub.com

ISBN: 978-93-5744-474-3

First edition 2022

DEDICATION

For those people who loved me, pushed me, championed me, reviled me, rejected me, and most importantly, held me when I needed it most.

ACKNOWLEDGEMENT

To Mum, Dad and Katrina. My first audience. You always have and always will be my best advocates and greatest support. Thank you for giving me life and sustaining it ever since.

Sam, I love you for helping me to dream bigger and believe that I will see those dreams become reality. Thank you for being on my team.

Thank you, Therese, for prophesying my poetic ventures, amongst everything else you do. My sister, you know these stories as well as I do.

To Jennie, thank you for holding me as I leapt from one life into the next, and steadying me each time I wobbled. You always remind me of the light.

Louise, I couldn't have finished this without your effervescence and your conviction. Thank you.

Finally, to God. For Your glory. I owe all of who and what I am to You.

PREFACE

These poems were written during one of the most tumultuous, yet invigorating seasons of my life. Suddenly, I found myself in a period of transition, with everything in my life up in the air. I was between the old and the new, the known and the unknown. It was painful and raw, but there was also beauty in the midst of uncertainty. I came to learn who I am again. These poems were my catharsis. They are imperfect and simple, and written for myself. Nevertheless, I am proud of them, for they are a testament to the parts of myself and my life that have got me to here. So, if you are reading them, be gentle, as I have learned to be.

Refining

I have walked through the fire,
but it did not consume me.
I expected desolation, destruction, obliteration
(As did you, who struck the match,
who set the fire,
and watched it burn all around me).
Sure, it burned and it singed as it flickered and
flared.
The smoke was a plume that could have
suffocated alone.
Yet -

What I found in its centre was not the end of all,
but the start.
A burning, enflamed heart.
A knowing, deep in my own core.
This was a purifying, refining blaze.

The flames that were meant to swallow me,
struck off every inch of mud slung my way:
every hurt, disappointment, grudge, every
weight that was bearing down on me.
The ashes of my former self,
mixed with the tears of every moment come
before,

until I emerged...

A new woman.
A new creation.
A phoenix, rising.
Clean, pure, free.
With nothing left but embers and empty hands,
I realised I possessed everything.

Bridal Shower

The bride to be wore flowers,
and the sun shone only for her,
while I stood in the shadows,
mystified by her radiance.
She floated around the room,
with the grace of every true lady there ever was;
with a tender, secret smile tucked up on her lips,
and a twinkle in her eye that sparkled just for her
beloved.

My heart ached -
knowing at 20 her life was merely beginning,
and she had not had to wade through the same
dark waters
or plod the same lonely road,
that 30-year-old, single me had for so long.

It was not the romance that caught the lump in
my throat,
or caused the misstep and stumble in my toes,
or the hollowness in my smiling eyes.

My heart ached for the life not yet lived,
and perhaps may never be.

Perhaps the quantum leap from the pages of my
mind,
to the pages of reality's history books and photo
albums,
would never be.

I ached for the simple joys of a life shared.
A kind word over tea and toast in the early
morning sun.
The hand held as I walked the street.
A warmth on the other side of the bed.
The lightest of touches communicating the
deepest of knowings.

In that sweet room,
full of gracious women,
the very picture of beauty, love and magic,
I felt my heart twist
and the familiar throb of hope lost
and time passing by.
Soon I would be a husk, never to hold a new life.
My gaze found the bride to be,
adorned in white and gold.
As her hair shimmered in the glory of the
afternoon light,
I held myself closer,
with the thought that,
'one day, this could be me'.

Playground Philosophising

'Higher, higher,'
comes the call from her tiny frame.
Pushing her weightless body, I submit.
Looking for threats to her security
in this metal and rubber chariot of dreams.
Watching her wispy golden-brown ponytail
flying featherlike and high in the breeze behind
her.
Her miniature spotted shoes pushing for the sky.

'I'm in the tree, I'm in the tree.'
Every statement in repeat;
doubly enthused, doubly exclaimed.
Her magical mind transports her far beyond the
swing set,
to places beyond her reality.
The slippery dip is more than a slide,
but a rollercoaster of theme park proportions,
or a portal into a new world.
Her dinosaur jumper and tulle skirt the uniform
of an intrepid adventurer,

leading her into jungles and deserts and
imaginary lands.
And I, along for the ride.

'Again, again!'
I take up the gauntlet,
of bringing forth more giggles and smiles,
of keeping this courageous toddler
pleased and entertained -
a court jester at work.
She is on a simple quest;
for joy, for amusement.
And though I know I am here to be the
chaperone,
I also know I am here to learn.

Mondays

Monday.
I used to rush, knowing I would sit in a meeting
simply for the sake of a meeting.
When the coffee was stronger,
and the blows hit harder.
When there was a simultaneous freshness in the
air,
and a communal resistance at all that was not
weekend.
The dreary faces of colleagues and pupils alike,
as they launched back into rhythm and routine.
The conversation about the weekend just gone
bringing alight the eyes with memories
of rest, Saturday sport, and city escapades;
whilst dulling them with the thought of
the next 5 days before one would taste freedom
again.
Living Monday to Friday,
with Saturday and Sunday
firmly in the mind's eye.
The weight of the week's work
bearing down on your shoulders.

Now, Monday is different.
Monday is free.

Monday is full of possibility.
Monday is a blank canvas.
Monday is space.

Monday is light streaming through the window,
while I lay in my news sheets and my sage quilt,
basking in the light touching my face,
rolling side to side.

Monday is long walks along the coast,
with the sea breeze on my skin,
and a sweet friend at my side,
taking our time as we take in the endless ocean.

Monday is whiling away the hours,
in a comfortable corner,
admiring the passersby
and luxuriating in velvety words from a new
novel.

Monday is watching television on the lounge,
with not another care in my mind,
enjoying the feeling of the cushions
creating a nest for my once weary body.

Monday is drinking it all in and taking time out.
Monday is me day.

Abba

You see me for all my cracks and chips and
flaky bits,
and you choose me anyway.
You see all the harsh, rough, exposed parts,
and you hold me still.
You know every mistake I've ever made, and
every way I've fallen short,
and you honour me all the more.

You are at your best, when I am at my worst,
for you love to mystify with your choices and
actions, and you never do what I expect you to
do.
Where I deserve reprimand and rejection,
you give me kind words and draw me in closer
and tighter.
Where I deserve shame and guilt,
you give me acceptance and joy.
Where I deserve disowning and casting off,
you call me daughter again and again.
I am risen up when you should let me fall.

I am undone by your goodness and your
graciousness.

I am brought to tears,
when my spirit recognises your hand at work.
I am brought to my knees,
when my heart is filled with your mercy and
compassion.
I am risen up when you should let me fall.

All around me is the evidence of who you are
and how you move.
And it is not lost on me, that you,
you who could choose separation,
distance, impartiality,
you choose face to face,
forehead to forehead,
breath to breath.

In your presence, I come alive.
At your voice,
I quake and shudder with the immensity of what
you say.
At your touch,
I melt with the peace and warmth of your
tenderness.
At your look,
I blaze and smoulder with the fierceness and
empathy.

You're more than I could ever hope to have
known,

and my whole existence is for yours.
I will never have enough to give you in return.

There has to be a response.
What comes out of me when I allow you in,
is a tumble of love and gratitude,
or praise and tears.
My body moves in ways I cannot control.
My mouth speaks words I cannot recognise.
My mind reaches peaks I never knew existed.
I have to pour out all that I have and all that I
am,
just to bring you a scrap of what you've given
me.
I may look crazy in the eyes of the world,
but this immeasurable, intangible gift
is worthy of it all
and so much more.

Everyday Magic

There is a sparkle in the everyday
that was once dismissed or taken for granted;
but now that we have been confined,
it glitters like the magic it truly is,
and has always been.
We just have new eyes to see and sense it now.

The exhilaration of the everyday is beyond
what one could feel on a rollercoaster or a
skydive.
The moment you drive from your suburb to the
bay,
and you hit 70km/h, feel the road opening up
before you.
It is more than you could have asked for
on a bright Saturday morning.

The way the day ambles towards nightfall.
The hush of dusk when the families have gone
indoors
because daylight saving ended weeks before.
The calm indigo that settles over the sky and the
surrounds.

There are flowers still growing,

and the sun is still shining,
and you are still ageing.
But how will you take each day?
Will it be a full moment of grace,
or a wasted, miserable stretch of time?

When you look up and appreciate the sky for
what it is --
the dome of your existence,
that brings peace and infinity,
but also underlines your obscurity and tininess.
Then you will know that you are still living
and breathing.

Book Club

I have always dreamed of this,
a space and a place and a few familiar faces,
in which to share the delight of what
Jane Austen called
the 'enjoyment of reading' and
the 'pleasure in a good novel'.

And so, we gather, fresh hopes and finger food
on the coffee table, each with, not a copy of the
so-called masterpiece, but...
a phone and an audiobook?
I place down my battered, pencil inscribed
paperback, aware that my notes seem
painstakingly meticulous, verging on excessive.
But I am a cheat,
for these are not the notes of an overzealous
reader; they are the work of four turns around
the HSC-sun,
inscribing the thoughts, explanations, and
literary devices for my weary students to soak
up and spit out
in their stock-standard, sub-par,
three-body-paragraph essays.
So I am not a novice to this work,

and I did not take pleasure in this memorable
novel at first.
Nevertheless, I am here and eager to please.

The circle is complete,
with our hosts taking their tea and their seats
and surprisingly bearing whiskey.
'What comes next,' I wonder in anticipation,
for I have always hoped for comrades on this
endeavour to devour as many delicious stories as
I possibly could.
I did not find it among my peers,
I did not find it in my students,
but perhaps today, in this fire-warmed room,
I will ignite the flame that has been flickering
for companions.

'Let's talk about the fact that none of these
characters have their act together,'
one boldly declares,
and we're off,
launching into the deep of the tale set before us
in digital and paper glory.
My heart races, as I recognise the thrill of
the quick-witted, fast-paced exchange of
thoughts, opinions, queries.
I sigh with agreeance, as they pinpoint
the nuanced notion I had long since held.

I nod along, encouraging this rigorous
exposition of the writer, the protagonist, the
structure, and the style.

'What do you think?'
They turn to me, expectant and eyes hopeful,
that I will have something meaningful or
humorous to contribute.
I gingerly flick the pages of the worn paperback,
thumbing the dog-ears and tabs.
I narrow in on my favourite chapter,
a tender and heartbreaking metaphoric passage.
Will I sound a fool or pretentious if I
invite them into my innermost workings?
Facing them all I begin,
with a leap of the heart
and an earnest suggestion.

Blackwood Beach

I am transfixed to my small cliff-top view,
as I gaze out to the ocean before me.
The sky is clear, blue to the horizon and beyond,
a perfect colour chart spectrum of shades.
The breeze whistles as it passes my ears,
whipping off the ocean and travelling back to the
streets and apartments.
I take in the rockpools, dotted with moss and
shells, a weathered, textured maze of wonders to
be discovered.
The gulls dance as they dive from the air.
My skin tingles from the warmth of the autumn
sun.
I watch the waves,
roll and roll and roll,
drifting seamlessly across my view,
before barrelling and breaking,
crashing on the rockface,
the foam spray rising up like a piece of art on the
brilliant cerulean backdrop.
I run my hand through the seagrass and spinifex.
Sunlight glints and glimmers off the perfect sea.
I am here,
and in this moment on Blackwood Beach,

I am more aware
of my smallness,
and yet still more
aware of my significance.
A recognition, a knowing in my soul and spirit,
of home,
and other mysteries of the ordinary.

The Hallway of Life

I am in the hallway,
the corridor of life.
I have closed one door behind me,
and am waiting for the next to open.

I am afraid. It was gruelling to get here,
to cross the threshold of the old and familiar,
and step into the beyond, not knowing what I
would find.

I had to cut ties and shed my skin,
and it was terrifying and liberating all at once.
I had to stare down the barrel of the gun
and stand my ground as I called their bluff.

Now that I am here,
I feel exposed and vulnerable,
as if I am naked in a crowded room.
I am kilos lighter than I ever was before,
all the baggage left at the door.

But this waiting is long and lonely.
For not everyone makes it through the mire
to the other side, and in this antechamber,

I am alone.
But I stand, battered and bruised,
ready for the new door to open.
Expectant and brave.

Sunday Sun

The Sunday sun has prevailed,
despite the dreary cloak of grey
that filled all we could see driving into this city
for the afternoon spectacle.
Our fortunes didn't appear favourable as we
arrived to the grey wash above.
But as we wandered from our riverside lunch
to the colosseum of coveted glory, it was as if
the football gods heard our silent but fervent
prayers and rearranged the elements just for us.

Through the turnstiles,
we jostled our way to door 113,
the atmosphere prickling with excitement,
energy bouncing off the beer-laden men
and women adorned in their team colours.
And I, I feel an imposter here.
My team jacket and membership tickets say
otherwise, though I confess my devotion is not
longstanding.
For the one who holds my hand through the
crowd is also the one who holds my heart,
and this - this is his boyhood dream.
So I have mustered all the enthusiasm I can

to stand in solidarity as his boys take on one of
their most-hated rivals.
My own parents are appalled by my betrayal,
switching the red and white for blue and yellow,
and the mighty dragon for the native eels.

As we pass down the steps,
I know I am on hallowed ground.
The field is fresh, the lights bright, and the
stands are bursting with pride and with cheers.
Our seats are close enough to smell the grass,
hear the awful smacks of player collisions,
heckle the sideline officials, and feel a part of all
the action.

Kick-off,
and the sea of spectators roar,
30 000 voices erupting, and the spell is cast.
All around me they are fixated,
a single focus on the forwards gaining ground
in their quest to reach the try line.
I look beside me, to the man who is still the
12-year-old,
cheering on his heroes,
full of hope and expectation, analysing each
play.
He is immersed, body and soul, and nothing I
could say in this moment would be powerful
enough to break this bond.

I stare up through the stadium roof,
as below the two teams go to battle, a clash of
titans, and I see the flossy sky, now awash with
golden pinks and blues,
and I feel it.
The nostalgic, instinctual response that says I am
part of something bigger than me.
I feel the content settle over me, a warmth
through my system,
and I rest back in my seat,
enjoying this Sunday sun.

First Day

New job jitters are filtering through my system
as I press '7' and wait for the little shuttle
in this gold-plated foyer, nestled amid the
Sydney sandstone.
The ghosts of convicts and colonial settlers of a
time long since passed feel nearby in the
cobblestone back alley and Yellowblock
structures welcoming me, an alien in this
landscape.
The tangle of old and new is as jumbled as my
nerves, as I listen for the elevator making its
slow descent to the ground floor, stepping side
to side, back and forth.

This was the leap of faith, and today it feels like
a cavern I shouldn't have crossed.
Doubt fills my fragile mind,
as I read the professional firms on the wall.
I have traded expertise for incompetence,
five minutes door to door for a train
amid the commuters in this hive of a city.
I don't know why I thought I could reinvent
myself or make it on the other side, where the
grass should be greener.
I have nothing but my once agile mind,

my cheerful smile, my nervous laugh,
and my pen to offer.

The doors open suddenly,
and I am inside the mirrored lift that will be my
rocket to triumph and prosperity or,
my casket in the grave of my career.
The elevator music is my only companion,
although delayed in arrival, as I journey closer
and closer to my new office.
I will be made or broken here.
I breathe in deeply,
the lift stops,
the doors open,
and here I am.

Walking the Line

I am torn between two worlds -
one is full of colour, dreams, imaginings,
of more than what can be seen with the naked
eye;
one is grounded firmly in reality,
where nothing is anything but what you can
discern sensibly.
I live with feet in both, and I feel the tension
pulling my body, spirit, soul back and forth.
I am a ragdoll flailing around, a tug-o-war in
substance.

My natural inclination is to pull down my hood,
plant myself in reality the gritty, messy,
mundane day to day.
The cynic in me wears the worries of the world,
the burdens become my coat full of rocks.
They snigger at those dreamers who occupy the
other world, peering down their noses in
condescension.
The world is shades of brown, with splashes of
colour, but the joys are tempered and rough.

The other is a world that feels alive and
dazzling,

like staring into the sun and everything else
becomes brighter.
I feel my feet lifting off the ground when I
inhabit this land,
a place where possibilities are the lifeforce,
hope in every encounter,
and every corner affirms and honours the virtues
that we hold within.
There is magic in the most unassuming of
people and places, and it is not absurd to
believe in each other,
believe in benevolence,
believe there is more.

I am moon-walking in zero gravity,
untethered and released,
or I am firmly grid-locked.
I know where my head, my heart,
my spirit belongs.

Don't Take Things So Seriously

'I have a feeling we'll have a girl,'
I say, with a little bit of hope.
'Then I'd just push you down the stairs,'
he replies with a casual laugh.
His joke does not bring forth the same easy
response in me.
This is a split-second decision between
fear and outrage and hurt.

Fear sees his smiling eyes and jovial
countenance, and all of a sudden, he is a
different man.
Eyes clouded over in a haze of rage and abuse,
a beer in one hand and the other raised to me,
ready to strike in a moment.
He is every man that I have had cause to plead
with, to watch out the corner of my eye,
to placate with words and my submission.

Outrage sees his relaxed stance and dismissive
gesture,
and he becomes every male figure,

who ever laughed at my expense,
or put me in a box, or said 'it's just a joke,
don't take things so seriously'.
Rage is ready to gauge his eyes and wound his
ego.

Hurt sees his demeanour and feels a wall go
back up, where it had been slowly brought
down,
and a crack in the solid trust that had been
forged between us.
A thorn in the heart that bruises and stings,
just as the men who taught me to feel
insignificant,
made me feel less than human,
ignored me, wounded me too.

All in a second, I am warring inside,
unsure of how to proceed,
knowing this joke was no joke to me,
though I am taking issue not with this man,
but the men before him.

I am afraid, I am angry, I am hurt.
I am all of these things, and still
there is something more...
I am disappointed that my secret fear,
that I will never be a mother at all,
that I'll never be loved enough,

has reared its head and been exposed.

I turn my face away, and let the tears gather in
my eyes.
Ready to roll on out, they are fearful, angry, hurt
tears, all in one,
bullets pounding the face of this shell-shocked
woman.
I have to get away before I retch with the pain or
lash out uncontrollably.

He reaches for me.
'It was just a joke.'
The chorus of every man who overstepped
before.

'Let me tell you all the reasons why that isn't
funny to me,' I begin.
I am decided.
Time for both of us to take this seriously.

Locked Down Life

I have felt the stillness of the city,
heard the silence of empty streets and full
homes.
I have paced these rooms as much as an inmate,
stared at the walls and ceiling, urging them for
their stories and secrets.
I have curled myself up more than my body
should allow,
to fit in the space on the lounge that is still
graced with sunlight.
I have stretched myself out, in surprise,
to find more space than I knew,
and this corridor as fitting a home gym as I ever
did see.
I made the easy commute to and from work
23 steps from bed to desk precisely,
though not a colleague in sight.
I found myself more often than not counting
down to 11, and waiting with bated breath for
the rising tide of numbers,
to hear our fate at Gladys o'clock.
I have run on a single petrol tank for an
impossible time,
and discovered a whole new world within 10km
of home.

I have found hidden stars in the walls,
and friends in the birds, who are still free to flit
from one abode to the next, and allowed to perch
for more than a pause.
I have yearned for family,
just to be able to see their faces not on the other
end of a screen, but at the end of my fingertips.
I have cried a river or three, and instead,
learnt to form family where I can.
I have traversed the footpaths and trails and
tracks, many a companion,
20, 000 steps a day just to be anywhere but in
this unit.
I have slept,
because sleep is not for the weak,
but for the locked down.
I has become 'we',
for this is a shared trauma,
though the coastline has dictated just how 'we'
we really are.
I have marvelled in the majesty of the natural,
and mourned the depths of my loneliness and
isolation.
I have longed for an end,
but am afraid of returning.
I have had nowhere to be except exactly where I
am.
What a double-edged sword,
this locked down life.

Not Broken, Whole.

You have tried to tell me who I am -
your words accuse, convict, condemn.
But I am not who you say I am.
You can paint me with your regrets, fears,
insecurities, guilt and shame.
It will not stick.
I am more than you ever knew,
and I paint with my own spectrum and brushes
now.

I waited for you to appreciate all the gifts I had
to offer,
had you only given me the space to share them.
I poured out all of myself for the sake of those
we held in our hands.
I thought I had given you all -
I couldn't have given any more.
I was running on empty for so long that I just
thought it was how we all live.
I dragged my body behind my will, crawling,
inching onwards.
You took it all,
and still it was not enough to fill your cup.
I gave you my sleepless nights, my rumination,
my weekends.

I gave you my creativity, my energy, my voice
and my hands.
I gave you my peace.
I even gave you my body, that I lay bare on the
altar of your worship.
It was never enough.
You took and took and took,
devouring me morsel by morsel,
all with my consent before I could know I'd even
given it.
Until all that was left to spit out
was the dry husk of my former self.
I thought I was broken because I had nothing left
to give.

Then I woke up.
I woke up and I threw out my hands and put my
foot down.
I drew a line in the sand.
You said you'd let me go.
You released me,
with barely a flinch or a blink of an eye.
I was at the edge of freedom,
ready to rebuild, restore, renew.
But you couldn't let me be,
so your last defence -
you flung your words at me -
your last attempt to hold the power.

But I am not who you say I am.
I am awake to your schemes and
I will no longer fall prey.
I am no victim, though you made me out to be
one.
I am not weak, though you would have me
believe it.

I am brave.
I am fierce.
There is a lion within, roaring loud and
unwaveringly.
For I know my worth now,
and I know the strength I've always had but
didn't recognise.
I am a new creation.
I rise like the phoenix, a beauty and wonder to
behold.
I have more within me than you could ever have
held.
You thought you broke me,
but I am kintsugi -
a vessel held together with gold -
more beautiful and strong than I ever was
before.
I carry light and joy.
I radiate wonder and hope.
You are insignificant,
for I am free.

Together and Apart

If I had known the last time would be the last,
I would have clung to you a little bit tighter,
drawing your imprint on my body,
so I wouldn't forget the feel of you, when you
hug me hello and goodbye.
I would have recorded every smile,
on the film of my mind, so I could replay them,
pause, replay over and again.
I would have captured every laugh,
bottled them up, held them close to my chest,
for each subsequent moment of anguish and
utter despair.
I would have held your hand,
just to study every wrinkle, every blemish, every
crease, so I would know it intimately by touch
alone.
I would have breathed deeply,
allowing your scent to fill the recesses of my
subconscious, to bring you back to me in an
instant.
If I had known I would have lingered at the door,
a final moment to drink in the look of you,
then once sneakily at the car door,
you standing on the veranda,

that loving, fractionally amused gaze.

I wouldn't have left if I'd known then what I
know now,
and I would be with you still.

Wonders of the World

There is so much more to see,
experience, and understand of the world,
and I find there is no end to the depth of awe and
wonder
I feel when I go to new places or see new things.
So I spend my time wistfully dreaming of past
discoveries and new adventures.

And yet, on days
like today,
I see my own little patch of this earth
with new eyes and realise there's plenty of
wonder left in this place.
It's not for the landmarks or the culture or any
other attraction.
It's the wonder of the people,
and I'm filled with pride, and my heart is
bursting,
and I'm overwhelmed with the kind of love that I
can't quantify or qualify.

And I remember what it feels like to be fulfilled,

and I stay.
And it doesn't feel like settling or a consolation prize,
but like choosing the thing that already chose me long ago.
It feels like coming home to the self I had forgot.

Waiting

I am in a tiny boat, cast out to the waves,
rocking perilously from side to side,
tossed about as the tide goes every which way.

All that stretches out around me is ocean.
I feel alone.
I do not know which way is up,
which way is forward.
Every tool of navigation is broken,
and my sense of direction is skewed.

I cannot go back to the safety of the shore,
and I cannot find my destination or my next
port.

All feels beyond repair.
All feels beyond my control.

It is too late for regret,
though I have all the time in the world,
to ruminate on this choice, and this place.

I am afraid that as I sit here,
with time passing as always,

I am missing the opportunities waiting to be
caught.
All the things I am meant to be doing with this
life, merely possibilities.

I am where you have asked me to be.
I would not have chosen this for myself;
because I trust you, I am here.
If I am swallowed whole by the endlessness,
none could say I wasn't obedient,
for I will have been consumed in your name.

Then you get into the boat.
You are with me once more.

All that time waiting is insignificant.
The horizon comes into view,
though it matters not where I go anymore,
but simply that you are with me.
The seas are still turbulent,
but the tempest is of no consequence,
in your ever-presence.
There is hope in that horizon,
in that ray of sun breaking through,
and in your steady hands and compassionate
eyes.

You whisper unmistakably,
'You are the captain of the seas'.

I am not the helpless wretch, at the mercy of my
circumstances.
I am the master and captain,
with greater voyages ahead.
You and I at the helm,
we set a course.

You and I

You have come into my world,
and shown me that which I couldn't see
alone.
You have come with colour, light, laughter,
kindness.
You have come with a big heart,
and a bigger smile, ready to share them just with
me.

You are more than I could have imagined,
and better yet, because you are not a figment of
my mind,
but a living, breathing, real body and soul.

I never thought I would find home with another.
That is what you are.
Even when the waves of chaos and uncertainty
toss me about,
the innate knowing within speaks peace,
for in you I am home.

Before there was you,
there was me.
'I', 'me', 'my'.
Now there is 'us' and 'we'.

Before you, I was not wretched and incomplete.
I did not wander the world with a limp and a
missing piece.
I was whole as I was,
a full life and a full self.
Yet, in my deepest, quietest corners,
I felt that there had to be more.
There was a sliver of something icy and harsh,
that twisted and pulled at my core every time
I watched newlyweds dance,
or couples embracing in airport terminals,
or hands being held.
Knowing I could not reach out and grasp a hand,
for there were none yet made for me.
Every joy, every good and perfect thing,
was tempered by a sinking feeling,
and an awareness that there was something I
might never know in what I saw.

You came into my sphere and I found,
not my other half, but the extras that added to
my whole,
that made me something even more.
You turned up the lights that were set to dim,
you stoked the fire that was already burning,
you added vibrancy to the spectrum I was
already painting with.
You made every part of my existence more.

With you by my side,
I am most me.

Metamorphosis

The darkness is full.
Sound no longer exists, in this chasm, except the
pounding of her own heart.
Light and colour are merely echoes of an old
world,
a time before, if one ever really was.
It is swallowing her whole.
She cannot remember how long she has been
here,
where she came from, or how she came to be
here in this cocoon.
She and the blackness are one and the same.
It has been struggle and pain and saying
goodbye to all that she had.
No more the life she knew.
All she knows now is here.
Memories come and go as the tide,
they shift and fade as freely as dreams,
in this long, long night.
This is a death, to self, to the past, to control.

Something within,
the still small voice,
suddenly speaks.
'It is time.'

Push.
She does, knowing without knowing how or
why.
Crawl.
The light is near, and she must reach it, however
long she has to fight.
Break.
She is not breaking, though she feels it in every
movement.
She is breaking free.

Doubt plagues her.
Wrestling is worse than the dark.
She has been long cocooned in the safety of the
chrysalis,
safe and still,
in the obscurity.
Could this possibly be worth the battle of
transition?
Why leave this world for the unknown of the
next?
The discomfort of breakthrough is unlike any
other, until -

She emerges.
Flooded with sensations she was starved of for
so long.
She takes in the world through a new lens;

perspective born of deprivation and struggle and
determination.
There is colour and light again,
and that brilliance is both
around her and within her.
She is luminous.
Surrender leads to freedom.
This time not giving in or giving up,
but in surrendering to the process,
she finds herself again.
Upon examination, she is not the same.
Where entered a caterpillar, a butterfly is now
released.
Wings expanding,
ready to take flight, her horizons opening out
before her just the same,
she recognises that this was no mere transition,
not a simple shift,
but a total transformation.
Her metamorphosis.

I Am Who I Am

You are the light in the darkest moment of my night.

You are streams of living water in the desert of my day.

You are my deep well of joy, that will never run dry.

You are the voice that cuts through the crowd in my mind.

You are the rhythm that beats from my chest.

You are the breeze that refreshes my skin as it kisses my face.

You are the silence that speaks louder than words.

You are the arms I fall into that feel like home.

You are all to me and for me.

You. Are. All.

www.ingramcontent.com/pod-product-compliance
Lightning Source LLC
LaVergne TN
LVHW021249200726
843509LV00012B/1607